THE OFFICIAL ANNUAL 2021

WRITTEN BY STEVE BARTRAM
DESIGNED BY DANIEL JAMES

A Grange Publication

©2020. Published by Grange Communications Ltd., Edinburgh, under licence from Manchester United Football Club. Printed in the EU.

Photography © MUFC.

ISBN: 978-1-913578-00-8

CONTENTS

WELCOME TO THE 2021 MANCHESTER UNITED ANNUAL!

"Football without fans is nothing", as legendary United manager Sir Matt Busby once said. So, finishing the 2019/20 season in empty stadiums because of lockdown was a new experience for the Reds, but with the team bang on form when the campaign restarted in June, and the forwards Anthony Martial, Mason Greenwood and Marcus Rashford knocking in the goals, Ole's side climbed the table and ended up in third place in the Premier League and reached the semi-finals of the Europa League, the FA Cup and the Carabao Cup.

In these pages, you can relive not only the unique 2019/20 campaign and how United as a club coped with the challenges of lockdown, but also celebrate our return to the Champions League by revisiting our greatest-ever nights in the competition.

Examine the impact of our Portuguese magnifico, Bruno Fernandes, the evolution of top scorer Anthony Martial, and read up on the profiles of several of their Reds team-mates, then learn who their heroes were when they were growing up.

2019/20 was also an impressive year's work for MU Women. We're joined by skipper Katie Zelem to introduce Casey Stoney's entire squad, while Dutch international star Jackie Groenen provides an exclusive, uplifting piece for anybody – young or old – who needs inspiration.

There's all this and plenty more besides in the 2021 Manchester United Annual, including a wide variety of quizzes and brainteasers to tax your knowledge of all things United, plus the chance to win a Reds shirt signed by first team squad members!

Football without fans is nothing so remember to keep the Red flag flying high, wherever you're watching from…

2019/20
REVIEWED

With an unexpected three-month break in action due to the global pandemic, the 2019/20 campaign was certainly a unique season, and one full of memories. Here's how it all unfolded…

PREMIER LEAGUE

3RD PLACE

There were highlights galore in a league campaign which saw the Reds improve hugely on the previous campaign's sixth-place finish. The 4-0 mauling of Chelsea at Old Trafford raised expectations on the first day of the season, but mixed results in the opening months ruled out any realistic hopes of challenging for the title. Nevertheless, league leaders Liverpool should have been beaten but for a late equaliser in October, while December's successive 2-1 victories over Tottenham and Manchester City showed that that the Reds were capable of beating any opponent on a given day.

After the Premier League's first-ever winter break in February (and following the signing of Bruno Fernandes), Ole Gunnar Solskjaer's side set off on a barnstorming run, winning at Chelsea in the league for the first time since 2012 and completing a derby double over City with a memorable March win at a rain-soaked Old Trafford just before lockdown. After the break, the Reds' run of six wins and three draws in nine post-lockdown games was sensational, and crucially included a dramatic last-day win at Leicester City which secured a third-place finish and a spot in the 2020/21 Champions League.

With Marcus Rashford and Anthony Martial at their deadly best, Mason Greenwood making waves with an unbelievable first full season at senior level and new signings Bruno and Daniel James supremely influential in their debut campaigns, United's goalscoring improved vastly compared with 2018/19. At the other end, the defence also tightened up massively following the arrivals of Harry Maguire and Aaron Wan-Bissaka, meaning the Reds could reflect satisfactorily on some major steps in the right direction in the Premier League.

FA CUP

SEMI-FINALISTS

Ultimately, frustration and heartbreak awaited at Wembley Stadium as the jaded Reds were overcome by Chelsea in the semi-finals, but there were plenty of positives along the way. Juan Mata's neat chip settled a tight two-part third round tie with Wolves, before a 6-0 romp at Tranmere in which United were 5-0 up at half-time. Derby were also swatted aside, 3-0, and Norwich were overcome by Harry Maguire's extra-time winner in a 2-1 success at Carrow Road. The semi against Chelsea came amid a packed run of fixtures in which the Premier League had to be prioritised, but the Reds still picked up some invaluable experience of knockout football.

LEAGUE CUP

SEMI-FINALISTS

It took a nervous penalty shootout to overcome Rochdale at Old Trafford in the third round, but Marcus Rashford's double – including an unbelievable 30-yard free-kick – made for an unforgettable fourth round win over Chelsea at Stamford Bridge. Colchester were then brushed aside in the quarter-finals before a tough last four draw against Manchester City ultimately ended at the semi-final stage. Having lost 3-1 at home in the first leg, the Reds narrowly exited despite Nemanja Matic's second-leg winner at the Etihad Stadium.

EUROPA LEAGUE

SEMI-FINALISTS

Drawn alongside AZ Alkmaar, FC Astana and Partizan Belgrade in the group stage, Ole's Reds secured qualification with two games to spare after three wins and four clean sheets in the opening four games. In the knockout stages, Club Brugge and LASK were both heavily beaten, 6-1 and 7-1 on aggregate respectively, before the rejigged tournament took on a single-leg format in Germany from the quarter-finals. FC Copenhagen were overcome in extra-time thanks to Bruno Fernandes's penalty and an eighth clean sheet in 11 Europa League outings, but the Reds ultimately exited to Sevilla in the semi-finals. Three of Ole's Reds were to be named in the Europa League Squad of the Season: Bruno Fernandes, Fred and Marcus Rashford. Well done, lads!

THE KEY STATS

MOST STARTS

1. HARRY MAGUIRE — 55
2. VICTOR LINDELOF — 46
3. AARON WAN-BISSAKA — 45
4. DAVID DE GEA — 43
5. ANTHONY MARTIAL — 41

MOST GOALS

1. ANTHONY MARTIAL — 23
2. MARCUS RASHFORD — 22
3. MASON GREENWOOD — 17
4. BRUNO FERNANDES — 12
=5. SCOTT MCTOMINAY — 5
=5. ODION IGHALO — 5

MOST ASSISTS

1. ANTHONY MARTIAL — 12
2. MARCUS RASHFORD — 10
3. BRUNO FERNANDES — 8
=4. DANIEL JAMES — 7
=4. JUAN MATA — 7

PLAYED: 61
WON: 33
DRAWN: 16
LOST: 12
SCORED: 112
CONCEDED: 51

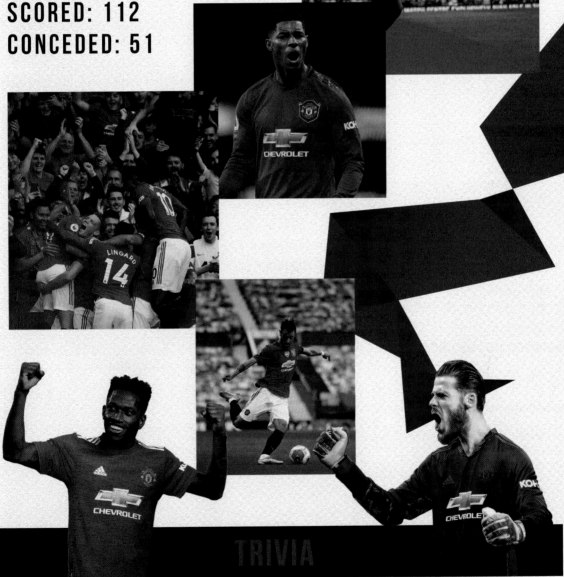

TRIVIA

BETWEEN JANUARY'S DEFEAT TO BURNLEY AND THE FA CUP SEMI-FINAL EXIT TO CHELSEA IN JULY, OLE'S REDS EMBARKED ON A 19-GAME UNBEATEN RUN — THE LONGEST UNITED HAVE HAD SINCE SIR ALEX FERGUSON'S RETIREMENT.

DAVID DE GEA

1

GOALKEEPER

**BORN: 7 NOVEMBER 1990;
MADRID, SPAIN**

The 2019 announcement of a new long-term contract for David De Gea was a massive signing for United, who have been indebted to the Spaniard's form ever since he arrived at Old Trafford in 2011. Now one of the most senior players in the Reds' squad, De Gea has long been accepted as one of the very best goalkeepers in world football.

UNITED CAREER IN NUMBERS

OVER 400 APPEARANCES
FOUR MAJOR HONOURS
(PREMIER LEAGUE, EUROPA LEAGUE, FA CUP, LEAGUE CUP)
FOUR SIR MATT BUSBY PLAYER OF THE YEAR AWARDS

> "
> ## THE IMPROVEMENT IN DAVID SINCE HE CAME TO UNITED IS HUGE – HE'S BECOME ONE OF THE BEST PLAYERS IN THE WORLD!
> "

PETER SCHMEICHEL | GOALKEEPER 1991-1999 | 398 APPEARANCES

TOP MOMENT IN RED

DURING OUR 3-1 WIN AT ARSENAL IN DECEMBER 2017, DAVID MADE 14 SAVES – A JOINT PREMIER LEAGUE RECORD FOR THE MOST SAVES IN A GAME!

MOST LIKELY TO...

SHOCK AN ENTIRE STADIUM WITH UNBELIEVABLE REFLEXES.

HARRY MAGUIRE 5

CENTRE-BACK

 **BORN: 5 MARCH 1993;
SHEFFIELD, ENGLAND**

It took Harry Maguire just 29 appearances in his first season at Old Trafford to convince manager Ole Gunnar Solskjaer to make him the new official club captain. "Everything about him tells me he is a leader," said the Norwegian. Harry joined from Leicester City in the summer of 2019 and quickly became a first team fixture with his dominant displays in central defence.

DID YOU KNOW?

HARRY PLAYED EVERY SINGLE MINUTE OF UNITED'S PREMIER LEAGUE SEASON IN 2019/20, BECOMING THE REDS' FIRST OUTFIELD PLAYER TO DO SO IN 25 YEARS.

> HARRY'S TERRIFIC. HE'S COMFORTABLE ON THE BALL, HE'S DOMINANT IN THE BOX AND HE'S EXACTLY THE TYPE OF CENTRE-BACK THAT MANCHESTER UNITED NEEDED.

GARY PALLISTER | CENTRE-BACK 1989-1998 | 437 APPEARANCES

TOP MOMENT IN RED

HAVING EXCELLED DEFENSIVELY ALL GAME, HARRY SCORED A TOWERING HEADER AT STAMFORD BRIDGE IN FEBRUARY 2020 TO GIVE THE REDS A 2-0 VICTORY WHICH WOULD PROVE CRUCIAL IN FINISHING THE SEASON IN THIRD SPOT.

MOST LIKELY TO...

CLEAR THE DANGER WITH A BOOMING HEADER UPFIELD.

HEROES TO HEROES

United's stars reveal which players they admired most when they were growing up!

> ## WHEN YOU LOOK AT THE CLASS OF '92, WHO WOULD HAVE THOUGHT THAT EIGHT OR NINE PLAYERS FROM THE SAME AGE GROUP WOULD GET THROUGH TOGETHER? IT'S AMAZING.
>
> A lot of those guys were my idols in my younger years, then it was Ronaldo coming through. For my position I'd always be looking at Ferdinand and Vidic. I thought they were outstanding as a partnership. They always had each other's backs, worked together brilliantly and they were great leaders as well.
>
> AXEL TUANZEBE

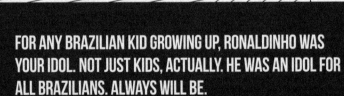

> ## FOR ANY BRAZILIAN KID GROWING UP, RONALDINHO WAS YOUR IDOL. NOT JUST KIDS, ACTUALLY. HE WAS AN IDOL FOR ALL BRAZILIANS. ALWAYS WILL BE.
>
> For me, he's the best player in the history of the game. I know there are players who have had better careers. Look at Zinedine Zidane, for example. His career was better, but in terms of purely footballing talent, Ronaldinho was better. He was more skilful. He was a top player who loved to party, and that made him an idol to all Brazilians. I don't think just Brazilians think this, I think a lot of people in football do, and I think as a player he had one of the biggest impacts on the sport. I can't overstate how big a hero he was – and still is – for so many people.
>
> FRED

I WOULD SAY MY FAVOURITE PLAYERS WERE THE BRAZILIANS, RONALDO AND RONALDINHO, BECAUSE THEY WERE BOTH FANTASTIC PLAYERS WITH BEAUTIFUL MOVEMENT AND GRACE.

They made their matches great to watch. I mostly loved Ronaldinho, because he was a player who could make you dream, with his great big smile on the pitch, with his great technical skills... I think that combination of great technical skills and the terrific goals he could score, it's that which inspires people.

ANTHONY MARTIAL

WHEN I STARTED TO PLAY FOOTBALL, AROUND 10 OR 11, MY IDOL WAS ZINEDINE ZIDANE.

At that time he was one of the best players in the world. I also really liked some players who played in Serbia, but if I have to choose one then it was Zidane. Zidane was my idol because he was playing the best football at that time. It's so hard to say for sure who is the best ever because there are definitely four or five players who can compete for that award. Cristiano Ronaldo, Messi, Ronaldinho, Zidane, Ronaldo, Maradona... it's hard to say who was the best of them all.

NEMANJA MATIC

HEROES TO HEROES

WHEN I WAS YOUNG, IT HELPED THAT ON A TYPICAL SCHOOL DAY, YOUR CLASSES WOULD FINISH AROUND 12PM AND YOU'D BE DONE FOR THE DAY.

I would go back and do my homework. Quick, quick, quick. Then I could go out into the back garden to play football. Just me, by myself, pretending to be players and saying things like: "It's Giggs on the ball." I loved it. There were loads of big players at the time but Giggsy was definitely the one who comes to mind straight away. It was just a fun thing to do as a kid. I would see him on the TV and try to copy his skills.

TAHITH CHONG

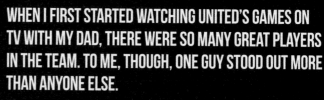

WHEN I FIRST STARTED WATCHING UNITED'S GAMES ON TV WITH MY DAD, THERE WERE SO MANY GREAT PLAYERS IN THE TEAM. TO ME, THOUGH, ONE GUY STOOD OUT MORE THAN ANYONE ELSE.

There was this player, younger than most of his team-mates, who was always showing everybody all his skills. He'd get kicked down but then stand back up and go again for the same defender who just kicked him. A lot of players get kicked once and just disappear from the game. Not this guy. He wanted more and more. Even more than that spirit, I loved the way he played, especially his shooting. The way he struck the ball, the way he shot from long-range, that's what always stood out to me because that's what I wanted to do as well. He could do everything, but most importantly he scored the kind of goals I wanted to score… actually, that's still what I want to do! That's why Cristiano Ronaldo was my footballing hero. That's why, when I would go out to play with my friends, I was like: I'm Ronaldo today. Even when I was training, I'd be thinking the same thing. I'd be shooting from far out, trying to do skills like Cristiano. I loved his stepovers, so I'd be trying them as well.

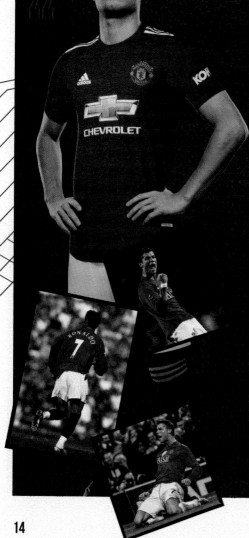

ANDREAS PEREIRA

WHEN I WAS YOUNGER, WE HAD A MARKET IN MY HOMETOWN IN SWEDEN THAT SOLD DIFFERENT SHIRTS THERE AND MY MOTHER BOUGHT ME A BARTHEZ SHIRT, SO THAT'S WHY I WANTED TO BE A GOALKEEPER.

I wanted to be a striker as well but, in that moment of my life, I wanted to be a goalkeeper.

VICTOR LINDELOF

GROWING UP, WAYNE ROONEY AND CRISTIANO RONALDO WERE THE PLAYERS I LOOKED UP TO — AND CARLOS TEVEZ WHEN HE WAS AT THE CLUB.

I didn't really speak to Cristiano as I wasn't in the first team then, but I've obviously spoken to Wazza. When I was about eight years old my uncle gave me a Rooney kit. As every kid does, when you're having a kickabout and you've got someone's name on your back, you just try to follow in their footsteps. I was a striker, so from that day, I wanted to be just like Rooney. And I wanted to play for England. He's given me advice. He's told me to stick to what I have always done, and just keep playing my football.

MARCUS RASHFORD

GIGGSY WASN'T A BAD PLAYER, WAS HE? WHAT HE DID AT MANCHESTER UNITED WAS AMAZING.

Every young winger looks up to a person like him. He was playing in the Premier League until he was 40 and he was still beating players. Credit to him, the way he looks after his body. It is amazing for me, when I go away on internationals, to learn from people like him. He is obviously someone I aspire to be like.

DANIEL JAMES

WAN-BISSAKA

AARON

29

RIGHT-BACK

**BORN: 26 NOVEMBER 1997;
CROYDON, ENGLAND**

Arguably the best one-v-one defender in the game, Aaron Wan-Bissaka enjoyed a brilliant debut campaign at United in 2019/20. Immediately his full-blooded tackling made Aaron a fans' favourite, and his form soon resulted in a first call-up to the senior England squad. The future looks very bright for the former Crystal Palace defender.

DID YOU KNOW

AT THE START OF HIS FIRST SEASON AS A RED, AARON STATED THAT HE WANTED TO TOP THE PREMIER LEAGUE'S TACKLING CHART AT THE END OF THE CAMPAIGN. HE ACHIEVED IT IN THE LAST GAME OF THE SEASON AT LEICESTER!

"

AARON WAN-BISSAKA IS A BETTER DEFENDER THAN TRENT ALEXANDER-ARNOLD. HE HAS SETTLED REALLY WELL AND WILL BE IMPORTANT IN THESE NEXT FEW YEARS.

"

GARY NEVILLE | RIGHT-BACK 1992-2011 | 602 APPEARANCES

TOP MOMENT IN RED

IN THE REDS' THRILLING MANCHESTER DERBY VICTORY AT THE ETIHAD STADIUM IN DECEMBER 2019, AARON BRILLIANTLY SHACKLED RAHEEM STERLING THROUGHOUT, TAKING THE MAN-OF-THE-MATCH AWARD IN A KEY WIN.

MOST LIKELY TO...

RECOVER THE BALL AND SEND A WINGER SPRAWLING WITH ONE OF HIS TRADEMARK TACKLES.

FOCUS ON

NEMANJA MATIC

MIDFIELDER

**BORN: 1 AUGUST 1988;
UB, SERBIA**

There are few cooler heads in the game than Nemanja Matic. Among his many honours, the experienced Serbian midfielder has won two Premier League titles with Chelsea and the Portuguese league with Benfica, so he knows what it takes to be part of a successful team. He brings high intelligence and great reading of the game to United's midfield whenever called upon.

DID YOU KNOW?

NEMANJA ISN'T THE ONLY FOOTBALLER IN HIS FAMILY — HIS BROTHER, UROS, IS A MIDFIELDER WITH QARABAG FK, THE REIGNING CHAMPIONS OF AZERBAIJAN!

I KNOW NEMANJA'S EXPERIENCE, PROFESSIONALISM AND LEADERSHIP WILL BE INVALUABLE TO THIS YOUNG, TALENTED GROUP. HE REALLY UNDERSTANDS THE VALUES OF PLAYING FOR MANCHESTER UNITED.

OLE GUNNAR SOLSKJAER | STRIKER 1996-2007 | 366 APPEARANCES

TOP MOMENT IN RED

ORDINARILY, NEMANJA'S BEST WORK IS DONE IN THE SHADOWS, BUT HE TOOK CENTRE STAGE IN MARCH 2018 WITH A BRILLIANT 25-YARDER TO BEAT CRYSTAL PALACE AND SECURE A 3-2 INJURY-TIME WIN AT SELHURST PARK.

MOST LIKELY TO...

WIN POSSESSION AND CALMLY FIND A TEAM-MATE AMID A CHAOTIC MIDFIELD BATTLE.

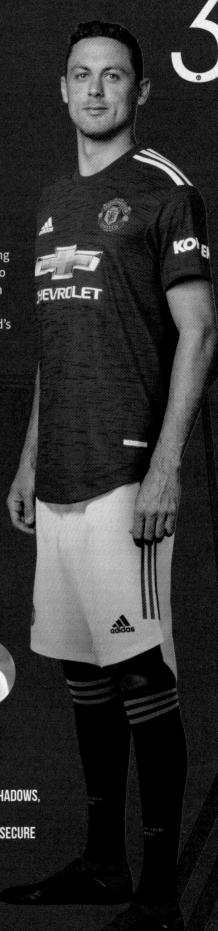

31

GAME CHANGER

SINCE HIS ARRIVAL IN THE 2020 WINTER TRANSFER WINDOW, BRUNO FERNANDES COMPLETELY TRANSFORMED UNITED'S FORTUNES. HERE'S HOW OUR PORTUGUESE MAGNIFICO DID IT...

"It's really good for me to be talked about alongside such names. But for me, Cantona was an amazing player for the club and I need to do much better to be compared with him," smiled Bruno Fernandes, having being told that his impact at Old Trafford was worthy of comparisons with that of the great Eric Cantona.

French striker Cantona arrived at Old Trafford midway through the 1992/93 season with United struggling to score goals. He solved that problem, inspired those around him and even prompted the entire squad to undergo a new kind of training regime, immediately leading to the Reds' first league title in 26 years. Cantona is credited with starting United's dominance of the 1990s and 2000s, so to bear comparison with him means you're doing something special.

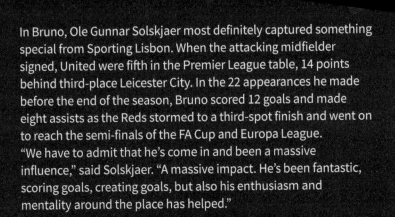

In Bruno, Ole Gunnar Solskjaer most definitely captured something special from Sporting Lisbon. When the attacking midfielder signed, United were fifth in the Premier League table, 14 points behind third-place Leicester City. In the 22 appearances he made before the end of the season, Bruno scored 12 goals and made eight assists as the Reds stormed to a third-spot finish and went on to reach the semi-finals of the FA Cup and Europa League. "We have to admit that he's come in and been a massive influence," said Solskjaer. "A massive impact. He's been fantastic, scoring goals, creating goals, but also his enthusiasm and mentality around the place has helped."

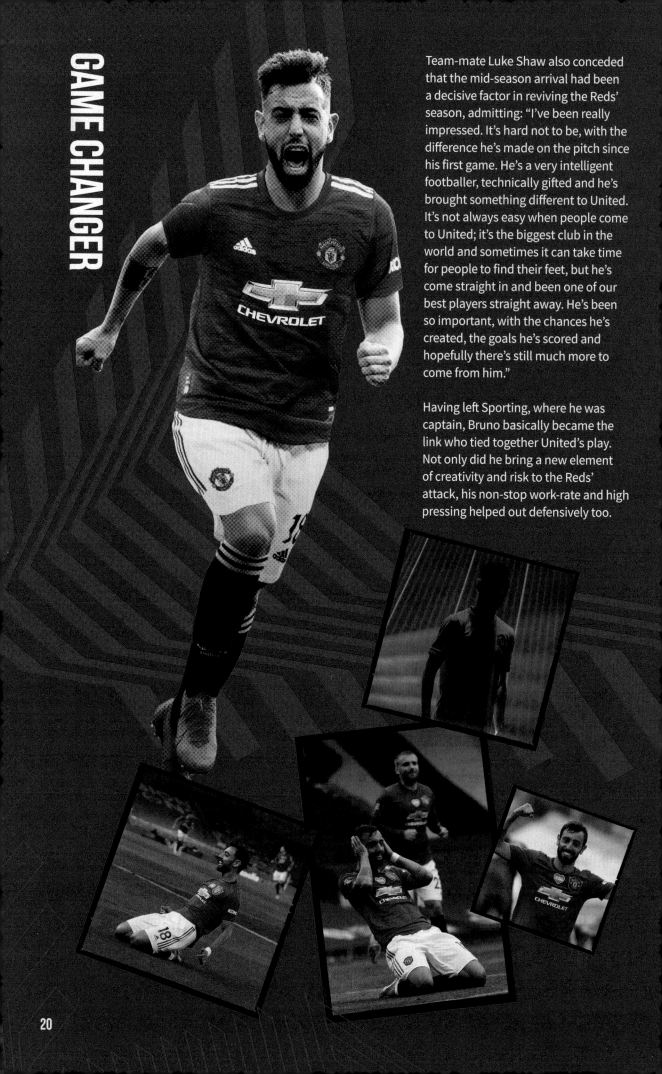

GAME CHANGER

Team-mate Luke Shaw also conceded that the mid-season arrival had been a decisive factor in reviving the Reds' season, admitting: "I've been really impressed. It's hard not to be, with the difference he's made on the pitch since his first game. He's a very intelligent footballer, technically gifted and he's brought something different to United. It's not always easy when people come to United; it's the biggest club in the world and sometimes it can take time for people to find their feet, but he's come straight in and been one of our best players straight away. He's been so important, with the chances he's created, the goals he's scored and hopefully there's still much more to come from him."

Having left Sporting, where he was captain, Bruno basically became the link who tied together United's play. Not only did he bring a new element of creativity and risk to the Reds' attack, his non-stop work-rate and high pressing helped out defensively too.

"I think that the most important aspect of my role is to help out my team-mates as best as I can," he said. "From a defensive point of view, I try to help them out when they need me to. When we lose the ball, I try to be the first one to react and to call on the other attacking players to help out in winning back possession. And, obviously, for me, to be able to build up the play, to have the ball and provide passes to my team-mates to enable them to score goals – it's very important.

"I think that's what I need to do a bit more because, yes, I've provided some assists but I think that I could have provided more, given the quality we have up front. Had they been provided better service, they would have scored more goals than they have so far, even though they've all had a great season and we combine really well together. "I believe that I can provide more assists, that I can improve on my numbers given the quality we have up front. I'm really happy for what I have done, but I'm not satisfied. Coming to Manchester is about winning trophies."

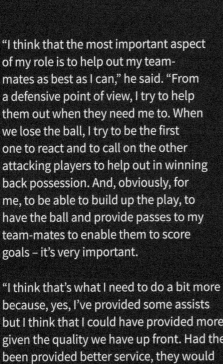

In addition to his huge variety of skills with the ball, Bruno's ambition has been a massive factor in his instant impact at Old Trafford, and a major reason he can be a big part of United's bright future.

FOCUS ON
PAUL POGBA

6

MIDFIELDER

**BORN: 15 MARCH 1993;
LAGNY-SUR-MARNE, FRANCE**

One of the world's most talented players and a key part of United's midfield. Paul Pogba is a superstar of the modern game, armed with a unique set of skills and a pedigree of years spent excelling in Italy and England, not to mention on the international stage with France. Paul is a one-off and an invaluable attacking weapon for the Reds.

TOP OF THE WORLD!

PAUL IS THE ONLY PLAYER IN HISTORY TO SCORE IN A WORLD CUP FINAL WHILE PLAYING FOR UNITED, FOLLOWING HIS KILLER THIRD GOAL FOR FRANCE IN THEIR 2018 TRIUMPH OVER CROATIA.

"
I PLAYED WITH PAUL AND I KNOW THE TALENT HE'S GOT. EVERYONE DOES. HE CAN DO EVERYTHING AS A MIDFIELD PLAYER — ABSOLUTELY EVERYTHING.
"

PAUL SCHOLES | MIDFIELDER 1994-2013 | 718 APPEARANCES

TOP MOMENT IN RED

IN APRIL 2018, PAUL SCORED TWICE IN TWO MINUTES AT THE ETIHAD STADIUM TO SPARK UNITED'S FAMOUS DERBY COMEBACK WIN OVER CITY; ONE OF THE GREAT THRILLERS OF RECENT SEASONS.

MOST LIKELY TO...

SEE AN OPENING THAT NOBODY ELSE CAN SPOT, THEN EXPLOIT IT IN STYLE.

SCOTT McTOMINAY

39

MIDFIELDER

 **BORN: 8 DECEMBER 1996;
LANCASTER, ENGLAND**

Another successful product of the United Academy, Scott McTominay has proven himself to be a fierce, athletic presence in the heart of the Reds' midfield since he broke into the senior squad at the end of 2016/17. A die-hard United fanatic, he drives the team forward whenever selected and his sensational development was rewarded with a new long-term contract in 2020.

TARTAN WARRIOR

 THOUGH HE WAS BORN IN ENGLAND, SCOTT DECIDED TO PLAY INTERNATIONAL FOOTBALL FOR SCOTLAND; HE WAS ELIGIBLE BECAUSE HIS FATHER WAS BORN IN HELENSBURGH.

> " SCOTT DRIVES THE TEAM FORWARD AND TRIES TO MAKE THINGS HAPPEN. HE'S A LITTLE BIT OLD SCHOOL, HE'S GOT DRIVE, HE GETS ON THE BALL AND DOESN'T HIDE. "

DARREN FLETCHER | MIDFIELDER 2003-2015 | 342 APPEARANCES

TOP MOMENT IN RED

 IN THE REDS' FINAL PREMIER LEAGUE MATCH BEFORE LOCKDOWN, SCOTT BAGGED A SENSATIONAL 40-YARD EFFORT AT THE STRETFORD END TO CLINCH A MEMORABLE OLD TRAFFORD VICTORY OVER LOCAL RIVALS MANCHESTER CITY.

MOST LIKELY TO...

POWER HIS WAY THROUGH A MIDFIELD BATTLE AND GET THE UNITED FANS ROARING.

FORWARD FOCUSED

IN 2019/20, ANTHONY MARTIAL RECORDED HIS BEST-EVER TOTAL OF 23 GOALS IN A SEASON TO FINISH THE CAMPAIGN AS UNITED'S TOP SCORER. THE FRENCHMAN'S EVOLUTION HAS BEEN A JOY TO WATCH...

When Ole Gunnar Solskjaer arrived as United's interim manager in December 2018, experts quickly predicted that the Reds' strikers would feel a huge benefit from working with the Norwegian who, as a player, made his name as one of the club's deadliest finishers. It certainly seems that the forwards were paying attention, particularly Anthony Martial.

The French forward enjoyed his career-best goalscoring season in 2019/20, having made the permanent move from left-sided forward to a striker, and he attributed much of that success to his manager.

"Ole gives us forwards a lot of advice in relation to our positioning on the pitch, and we're glad to receive it," said Anthony. "It's important to keep learning new things, new elements that can widen your range of options and make you more efficient as a player when you're out there on the pitch.

"He has a lot of knowledge to share from being a top striker himself and that will help us as forwards individually, and as we move forward as a team. Frankly, playing as a striker, you're not there to make blinding passes or massive runs. I've come to understand that to score, you have to be obsessed, to be fixated on just that, scoring goals. That's how you enjoy yourself as a striker. That's not a choice — that's how it has to be."

FOWARD FOCUSED

The signs were there on the opening day of the season, when he bagged a clinical close-range effort against Chelsea, that Martial had evolved his game, and those hallmarks of a penalty area predator continued throughout the campaign. A delightful dink at Norwich, a superb solo effort against Partizan Belgrade, goals home and away against City, a brilliant glancing header at Chelsea, plus his first-ever senior hat-trick – United's first since 2013 – were among the highlights of a superb season's work.

Having struck up brilliant on-field combinations with Marcus Rashford and new signing Bruno Fernandes, Anthony's 23 goals matched the total of his previous two seasons combined. His manager, for one, was delighted.

"Anthony has made huge strides this season in many aspects of his game," Solskjaer grinned. "Physically, he is at the best level of his career. We know he can score worldies but I like him scoring the simple goals, when he is in between the posts. He's done that a few times. He's in the gym a lot working on his fitness and strength. I'm just looking forward to seeing him improve. There's more to come from him."

Defenders beware; you have been warned!

A host of former United stars had their say on Anthony during 2019/20…

"MARTIAL ALWAYS HAS AN EYE FOR HIS TEAM-MATES AND THAT'S WHAT SETS HIM APART FROM THE OTHERS. THAT'S WHY I THINK HE'S A WORLD CLASS PLAYER."
ROBIN VAN PERSIE

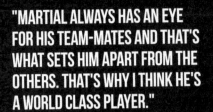

"EVERYONE'S GOT AN OPINION ON MARTIAL. HE'S A FERRARI. HE'S LOOKED LIKE A £100MILLION PLAYER."
OWEN HARGREAVES

"I LIKE HIM, I'VE ALWAYS LIKED HIM. I THOUGHT: WAS HE A NO.9, OR IS HE A WIDE PLAYER? HE'S TURNED HIMSELF INTO A NO.9 WITH EVERY GAME I WATCH, MORE AND MORE, SO IT'S GREAT TO SEE. HE'S TURNED HIMSELF INTO A PROPER NO.9. WHEN HE'S SQUARE-ON TO A PLAYER AND RUNS AT THEM, I THINK HE'S UNSTOPPABLE."
PAUL SCHOLES

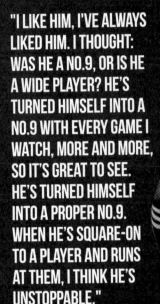

"HE LOOKS LIKE A DIFFERENT PERSON. HE LOOKS LIKE HE'S ENJOYING HIS FOOTBALL, HE'S CONFIDENT. YOU CAN SEE THE PICTURES — HE'S SMILING AGAIN. THIS GUY IS A DIFFERENT CHARACTER NOW UNDER OLE GUNNAR SOLSKJAER."
RIO FERDINAND

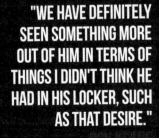

"WE HAVE DEFINITELY SEEN SOMETHING MORE OUT OF HIM IN TERMS OF THINGS I DIDN'T THINK HE HAD IN HIS LOCKER, SUCH AS THAT DESIRE."
ROY KEANE

"ANTHONY'S JUST GOT SO MUCH TALENT. HE HAS THE ABILITY TO BE GETTING OVER 20 GOALS SEASON IN, SEASON OUT — THERE'S NO QUESTION ABOUT THAT."
ANDY COLE

27

FOCUS ON

MARCUS RASHFORD

10

FORWARD

 **BORN: 31 OCTOBER 1997;
MANCHESTER, ENGLAND**

Our local hero made headlines in 2020 for becoming the charity saviour of hungry schoolkids around Britain, but he also enjoyed a major campaign on the field too. Finishing just one goal behind leading scorer Anthony Martial, the Wythenshawe-born star was often unplayable, and his rich blend of pace and skill, plus a growing hunger for goals, means he remains central to United's ambitions.

DID YOU KNOW?

FOR THE SENSATIONAL IMPACT OF HIS CHARITY WORK, MARCUS WAS GIVEN AN HONORARY DOCTORATE BY MANCHESTER UNIVERSITY IN 2020 — BECOMING THE YOUNGEST EVER RECIPIENT OF THE HONOUR!

> **RASHFORD COULD BE UP THERE WITH THE VERY BEST, 100 PER CENT, BECAUSE HE'S JUST GOT MAD TALENT.**

RIO FERDINAND | DEFENDER 2002-2014 | 455 APPEARANCES

TOP MOMENT IN RED

THERE HAVE BEEN SO MANY, BUT IT'S HARD TO TOP MARCUS'S 2019 INJURY-TIME PENALTY AGAINST PARIS ST GERMAIN, WHICH COMPLETED AN HISTORIC CHAMPIONS LEAGUE COMEBACK WIN. NERVES. OF. STEEL.

MOST LIKELY TO...

SPEED THROUGH A DEFENCE AND THUNDER HOME HIS FINISH.

FOCUS ON
MASON GREENWOOD

11

FORWARD

 1 OCTOBER 2001;
BRADFORD, ENGLAND

A one-off young talent, Mason Greenwood had his breakthrough season in 2019/20 and terrorised defences in both England and Europe. The teenager is one of the most naturally two-footed players to have represented the Reds, and his remorseless thirst for goals prompted huge hype almost as soon as he made his debut. He's so good already, but he's only just getting started.

THINKING OUTSIDE THE BOX

DURING 2019/20, MASON SCORED FOUR PREMIER LEAGUE GOALS FROM OUTSIDE THE PENALTY AREA — MORE THAN ANY OTHER PLAYER IN THE DIVISION!

> **MASON IS A DEFENDER'S NIGHTMARE. HE IS A FANTASTIC TALENT AND HE IS STILL ONLY AT A DEVELOPMENT STAGE; HAVING OLE THERE WILL GUIDE HIM ALONG THE WAY.**

DWIGHT YORKE | FORWARD 1998-2002 | 152 APPEARANCES

TOP MOMENT IN RED

AFTER THE PREMIER LEAGUE RESTARTED IN 2020, MASON RETURNED IN SENSATIONAL FORM - NEVER CLEARER THAN IN OUR 5-2 WIN OVER BOURNEMOUTH IN WHICH HE SMASHED HOME UNSTOPPABLE EFFORTS WITH BOTH FEET.

MOST LIKELY TO...

BAMBOOZLE DEFENDERS AND KEEPER, THEN PLANT THE BALL INTO THE NET.

HARD AT WORK...

The Reds' senior stars get put through their paces so they're always primed for action…

GRAFTING AWAY

The same goes for MU Women, who are always hard at work
behind the scenes…

ON THE RISE

Having stormed to promotion in 2018/19, their first-ever season as a professional club, Manchester United Women took on the top flight in 2019/20. Though the campaign was cut short by the coronavirus pandemic, Casey Stoney's side finished the season in fourth place, while also reaching the semi-finals of the Continental League Cup. With that experience banked and new signings in place for 2020/21, skipper Katie Zelem explains what the Reds' next steps need to be…

"I think fourth was a really good finish for us in our first season in the FAWSL. It was disappointing that the league had to end the way it did, but it was important for everyone's health and safety. Looking back, fourth is very good in our first season, plus we did particularly well in one of the cup competitions. We're always striving for better and there were some games where we dropped points when we shouldn't have, and that's the area where we could have improved. At the start of the season we said amongst ourselves that if Arsenal, Chelsea and City ran away at the top of the table, we wanted to be the best of everyone else and we achieved that."

"We had a few one-goal defeats against the top three teams and what we need to tidy up are sloppy goals we conceded and maybe some of the chances we missed. Those were the situations where you could see that the top three teams had more experience, so they were able to run away with a few more points.
It takes consistency to win the league and that's something we need to focus more on. We dropped some points which we shouldn't be dropping and, if we want to be challenging for the title, we just can't be doing that. We beat City and ran Arsenal and Chelsea close when we played them, so I think if we can keep our performances at that level through the season then we're in a really good place."

ZEL'S PROFILES

THE GAFFER: CASEY STONEY

I knew Casey before I joined United, having played with her at Liverpool, so I knew what sort of person she was and what kind of standards and values she holds. It's great that she demands such high standards – even when we win the game, she wants clean sheets and we go into every game with the mentality that we can always be better. For such a young team, that's great for us. We can't limit what we do. Casey's always striving for better for everyone around her and we couldn't ask for any more from her. She's never not working!

EMILY RAMSEY

1

"RAMBO IS A REAL GOOD PROSPECT. YOU CAN TELL JUST BY LOOKING AT HER THAT SHE HAS THE HEIGHT AND PHYSIQUE TO BE A WORLD CLASS GOALKEEPER. SHE'S BECOMING REALLY COMMANDING AND SHE ALSO BRINGS A LOT OF LIFE TO THE CHANGING ROOM."

22

FRAN BENTLEY

"ONE OF THE BEST GOALKEEPERS I'VE EVER SEEN WITH THE BALL AT HER FEET. SHE'S STILL SO YOUNG, BUT SHE PICKS PASSES THAT I THINK SOME OF THE OUTFIELD PLAYERS WISH THEY COULD PICK!"

MARY EARPS

27

"MARY'S VERY CONFIDENT IN HER PLAY AND I THINK EVERYONE COULD SEE THAT LAST SEASON. SHE MADE SOME GAME-CHANGING SAVES TO WIN US A LOT OF POINTS AND SHOW THAT IT'S NOT JUST ABOUT THE FORWARDS, AND I THINK THAT'S HOW SHE IS BOTH ON AND OFF THE PITCH."

MARTHA HARRIS

2

" THERE'S ONE WAY TO DESCRIBE MARTHA, AND THAT'S THAT SHE'LL RUN THROUGH A BRICK WALL FOR YOU. SHE'LL GIVE EVERYTHING FOR THE TEAM AND LEAVE NOTHING OUT THERE ON THE PITCH. "

3

LOTTA OKVIST

" LOTTA HAS A LOVELY LEFT FOOT AND I REALLY ENJOY PLAYING WITH HER. SHE'S SO CALM ON THE BALL, SHE'S SO NEAT AND TIDY AND ALWAYS KEEPS THINGS EFFICIENT, PLUS SHE'S A LOVELY GIRL OFF THE PITCH. "

AMY TURNER

4

" A LOT LIKE MARTHA, SHE'LL LEAVE NO STONE UNTURNED IN PURSUIT OF THE WIN. IF THERE'S SOMEBODY YOU DON'T WANT TO BE GOING INTO A 50-50 TACKLE WITH, IT'S AMY! "

> " ON THE BALL, SHE'S SO TECHNICALLY GIFTED. ABBIE IS ONE OF OUR CENTRE-BACKS WHO REALLY LOOKS TO PICK A PASS AND START THE ATTACKS FOR US. "

17 ONA BATLLE

> " ONA'S REALLY IMPRESSED US SINCE SHE JOINED IN THE SUMMER. WE NEEDED WHAT SHE BRINGS. SHE LOVES TO PLAY AND COMBINE, SHE'S SUCH AN ATTACK-MINDED PLAYER AND NONE OF US HAD REALISED BEFORE JUST HOW QUICK SHE IS! "

20 KIRSTY SMITH

> " LIKE ONA, SHE'S VERY CALM, VERY ATTACK-MINDED AND YOU CAN ALSO SEE THAT KIRSTY IS A VERY PHYSICAL PLAYER WHO'S SUPER FIT AND BRINGS A LOT TO THE TEAM BOTH ON AND OFF THE PITCH. "

MILLIE TURNER 21

> " THERE'S SO MUCH YOU CAN SAY ABOUT MILLIE, WHO'S A TOP DEFENDER. I'VE NEVER SEEN HER HAVE A BAD DAY, SHE LIGHTS UP EVERY ROOM SHE WALKS IN AND SHE'S A GREAT PRESENCE FOR US TO HAVE. "

10 KATIE ZELEM

" NOT MUCH TO SAY! I'M REALLY HAPPY WITH HOW IT'S GONE SINCE I JOINED IN 2018. THE CAPTAINCY WAS NEVER IN MY PLANS, IT WAS JUST ABOUT BETTERING MYSELF, SO WHEN CASEY ASKED ME IT WAS A HUGE HONOUR. I LOVE THE SQUAD, EVERYONE BRINGS SOMETHING DIFFERENT AND THAT'S WHAT MAKES THE TEAM SO SPECIAL. "

HAYLEY LADD 12

" WE CALL HER 'THE OCTOPUS' BECAUSE NO MATTER WHERE YOU'RE PASSING, SHE'LL STICK OUT ONE OF HER TENTACLES AND MANAGE TO INTERCEPT THE BALL. SHE'S THE QUEEN OF BREAKING UP THE OPPOSITION'S PLAY. "

JACKIE GROENEN

14

> JACKS BRINGS A LOT TO OUR GAME DEFENSIVELY. SHE'S VERY AGGRESSIVE WHEN SHE'S PRESSING, WHICH IS QUITE UNIQUE IN AN ATTACKING MIDFIELDER. SHE NEVER STOPS SMILING, SHE'S ALWAYS BUBBLING AROUND AND HAPPY.

16

LAUREN JAMES

> ONE OF THE MOST TECHNICALLY GIFTED PLAYERS I'VE EVER PLAYED WITH. LJ'S FEET ARE UNBELIEVABLE. SHE'LL BE IN THE TIGHTEST SPACE BUT SOMEHOW GET OUT WITH THE BALL. SHE'S GOING TO BE A VERY, VERY GOOD PLAYER AS SHE GROWS UP.

LUCY STANIFORTH

37

> I KNEW STAN BEFORE SHE JOINED, SO I KNEW HOW CLEANLY SHE COULD STRIKE A BALL. IN HER FIRST TRAINING SESSION SHE HAMMERED ONE IN THE TOP CORNER TO QUICKLY IMPRESS EVERYONE AND SET THE RIGHT TONE. SHE BRINGS IMPORTANT EXPERIENCE.

ELLA TOONE

7

> "TOONEY'S REALLY IMPOSED HERSELF ON THE TEAM, SHE'S SO DYNAMIC AND HER RUNS IN BEHIND ARE UNBELIEVABLE. SHE'S ALSO WORKED ON STRENGTHENING HERSELF, SO SHE'LL SEE THE BENEFITS OF THAT."

9

JESS SIGSWORTH

> "JESS SCORES PLENTY OF GOALS FOR US BUT BEYOND THAT, SHE'LL GIVE EVERYTHING FOR THE TEAM IN EVERY GAME, WHATEVER THE SITUATION. I LIVE WITH JESS SO WE'RE NEVER APART ON OR OFF THE PITCH."

LEAH GALTON

11

> "LEAH'S A KEY PLAYER FOR OUR TEAM. SHE BRINGS A LOT OF BALANCE TO THE LEFT SIDE. HER BALANCE AND POWER ARE PHENOMENAL, SO IT'S HARD FOR ANYONE TO KEEP UP WITH HER AND SHE GETS US A LOT OF ASSISTS."

IVANA FUSO

13

> SHE HAS UNBELIEVABLE FEET. IVVY LOVES DRIBBLING WITH THE BALL AND CAUSES A HUGE THREAT FOR US. WE DIDN'T HAVE THAT MANY DRIBBLERS BEFORE SHE ARRIVED SO SHE BRINGS A NEW DIMENSION TO OUR ATTACK.

18

KIRSTY HANSON

> KIRSTY HAS SCORED SOME CRACKING GOALS FOR US AND, LIKE JESS, WORKS SO HARD. SHE ALSO HAS THIS KNACK OF GETTING THROUGH ON GOAL WHATEVER THE SITUATION AND NO MATTER HOW MANY DEFENDERS ARE AROUND HER.

JANE ROSS

19

> LIKE AMY TURNER, SHE'S GOT SO MUCH EXPERIENCE AND IT'S GREAT FOR THE SQUAD TO HAVE THOSE VOICES AROUND. A LOT OF PEOPLE GO TO JANE FOR ADVICE AND SHE'S ALWAYS THERE TO HELP EVERYBODY, WHICH IS SO IMPORTANT.

EXCLUSIVE INTERVIEW
JACKIE GROENEN

The MU Women schemer could have had a career in judo or law, but she chose to play football at the highest level and is a star for the Reds. In this inspirational interview, she sets out the benefits of hard work, a variety of interests and the ability to follow your own instincts….

SO, JACKIE, HOW DID YOUR INTEREST IN FOOTBALL FIRST BEGIN?

I started out because my dad was a football player and so was my grandad. My dad was a bit upset that he got two girls when he wanted boys, but it was still kind of expected that we would start playing football, so we were all into football from the start! It's a family thing for us. I think at that time, whatever my sister was doing, I would try to do that as well, so when she started playing football I started up as well.

HOW BIG WAS GIRLS' FOOTBALL IN HOLLAND WHEN YOU WERE GROWING UP?

Back then, we were always the only two girls in the boys' team. It wasn't like now where girls can go and play with their friends for girls' teams; we always had to play for boys' teams. It was always me and my sister though, so we were fine together. It was always fun to see the opponents' reaction to us, because the boys we played with knew we could play football well and they were accustomed to it, but each time we played a new team, it would be: "Oh, look at that – they have girls in their team!" So back then it wasn't normal to be playing football whereas now, if you're in Holland, it's a very normal thing.

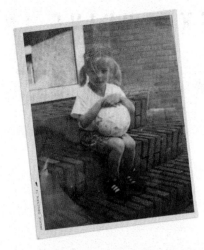

DID YOU ENCOUNTER ANY DIFFICULTIES AT THE TIME?

I was quite a dribbler, so if boys on the other team were annoying me during the game then I would dribble a lot because I would just want to show them. I would always push it a bit too far, so normally the coaches would have to pull me to the side and say: "Stop it. They're getting annoyed now, so it's time to play our normal game." But I loved to embarrass them if they had annoyed me before the game. The boys I played with at that time found it very normal that we were there, so they helped make it feel normal for us. I also felt like the team always had my back, so if we were getting into problems on the field then one of the boys would jump in and get involved. I suppose if you look back it was quite strange in the way that we always had to get changed in a corner somewhere, or a referee's changing room, because there was never anything arranged for us. It didn't feel weird to me at the time, but it was weird for a lot of clubs we faced.

WAS THERE A POINT WHERE YOU REALISED: THIS IS WHAT I WANT TO DO FOR A LIVING?

You know, not really. I think I was always jealous of the boys because I would say to them: "Oh, you guys are going to play in big, massive stadiums." Football for me was the thing I loved to do the most, but I never saw a career path in it. At that time it wasn't something you could touch or see, so I didn't even think about it that much. Even when I signed my first professional contract in Germany, not one part of me thought that this was going to be my career, this is what I was going to do for the next few years; it just felt like something I was rolling into. I would be lying if I said I was six and I wanted to play for the national team. I never really sat down and thought about that, I just played football because it was something that I wanted to do.

JACKIE GROENEN

AS WELL AS FOOTBALL, YOU COMPETED INTERNATIONALLY IN JUDO, YOU TOOK A LAW DEGREE AND LEARNT DIFFERENT LANGUAGES, SO YOU KEPT YOUR OPTIONS OPEN!

I started playing judo because my sister was doing it and although it was a hobby in the beginning, it kind of got out of hand! I started being very serious about it, playing tournaments all over the world, so when I had to drop it so that I could focus on my football, it was harder than I expected. I do like to do different things as well. I love to study. I love to make music once in a while too. I've just started playing the guitar and the girl who is teaching me has a band who I will go and play with sometimes. I basically just like doing things to take my mind off the routine, because being a pro athlete, you kind of go into your own little bubble. I've noticed that if I'm not careful then I can get sucked into that bubble and I don't know anything about anything else. When I'm in that place, my parents will say to me: "Have you seen what's happened here," about something in the world, and I'll just be oblivious to it. Doing different things gives me a way of stepping out of the bubble once in a while.

YOU WON THE EUROS, PLAYED IN THE WORLD CUP FINAL — WHEN YOU'RE LINING UP BEFORE THOSE GAMES, DO YOU THINK BACK TO THOSE TIMES AS A LITTLE GIRL WHEN PEOPLE SAID YOU COULDN'T PLAY FOOTBALL?

Yeah, I do. Sometimes the things that happen to me are very unrealistic, and I think I've always been a certain way because I don't really realise the size of what's happening to me until after I'm in the moment. But, one of the things that always blows my mind is when I see kids with my name on their shirts. For me that's crazy because when I was younger I wouldn't even think about getting a football shirt with a women's player on the back. That wasn't even a thing. So when I see it now, whether it's my name or one of my team-mates' names on their back, it's a moment where you realise: wow, these kids know what they want to be now. They want to do this. For me it was always Wesley Sneijder or Johan Cruyff on my back, but now I even see little boys with our names on their backs, and it makes me realise that the world has changed a little bit.

HOW MUCH HAS WOMEN'S FOOTBALL GROWN AND HOW FAR DOES IT HAVE TO GO?

It's still in a growing phase, but I like that I'm in the generation where I've seen both sides. I've played football before it took off for women and I'm playing it professionally now. When I play in a massive stadium now with lots of fans, I realise that I've also played in front of 10 people in the past, half of whom were my family! I'm really happy to be in this phase of women's football but, if it keeps growing as it is right now, in 10 years' time it'll have grown a lot more. I'm not saying it'll be as big as the men's game, but when I go out in Holland now or when I see men's players in Holland, you notice that the vibe has changed. They take us seriously now, they see us as athletes, which is fair because we put in the same effort. Five years ago that wasn't the case, so there has been a lot of progress made. Now that you have people like David Beckham taking it seriously and taking his kids to women's football, you know that the fanbase around the world will take it more seriously too. It can still step up but it's getting there.

WHAT ARE THE MOST IMPORTANT CHARACTERISTICS YOU'VE NEEDED TO BE SUCCESSFUL?

I always find this a hard question, but I do think that I'm very determined to get to where I want to be, so when I want something I do work really hard. I like to work hard, I enjoy it and if I've had a day when I've slacked off a little bit, I go to bed feeling uneasy. I always push it to the limits. The main thing for me is just that I've always done what I really like to do. It's a clichéd thing to say, but it definitely makes everything easier. I've always said to my parents that if there's a moment in my life when I realise that I don't want to do something anymore, I'm going to do something else, because I just want to do what I want to do. That makes training so much easier because it's what I want to do.

WHAT MESSAGE WOULD YOU GIVE TO ANY YOUNG GIRL WONDERING IF SHE CAN MAKE IT AS A FOOTBALLER OR IN ANY WALK OF LIFE?

I would say just make up your own mind. I feel like in a career – and that's not only football but across life – people are trying to make you go in certain directions, but sometimes you have to make the decision that feels right for you, even if it sounds stupid. I've not always made the most logical steps in my career, but that got me to where I am now. People used to say we were crazy. I was 15 and went to play in Germany. My parents would drive me three hours to and from training every day, and people just couldn't believe it, but I wanted to do it and it's led me to where I am. It's important, I think, to not always listen to people!

CHAMPIONS LEAGUE NIGHTS

In celebration of the Reds returning to the best competition in European football in 2020/21, we pick out United's top 10 nights since the Champions League began in its current format…

10 DEPORTIVO 0 UNITED 2

2001/02 QUARTER-FINAL, FIRST LEG

Having already lost home and away to the dangerous La Liga side in the group stage, United were underdogs when the sides met again in the quarter-finals. However, Sir Alex Ferguson's side were rampant and built a comfortable lead through David Beckham's cracker and a Ruud van Nistelrooy tap-in. The Reds were so dominant that 5-0 would have been a fairer score!

9 ARSENAL 1 UNITED 3

2008/09 SEMI-FINAL, SECOND LEG

Just 1-0 up from the first leg at Old Trafford, United made light work of burying Arsenal on their own patch. Ji-sung Park opened the scoring inside 10 minutes before Cristiano Ronaldo smashed in a 40-yard free-kick to all-but end the tie. In the second half, the Portuguese legend then capped a stunning counter-attack to render Robin van Persie's late penalty irrelevant.

8 UNITED 4 PORTO 0

1996/97 QUARTER-FINAL, FIRST LEG

Again, the Reds were underdogs against a Porto side tipped by many to win the Champions League. Instead, on an electric night at Old Trafford, United ran riot. David May and Eric Cantona struck in the first half, before brilliant counter-attacking goals in the second period from Andy Cole and Ryan Giggs rounded off one of M16's greatest-ever European nights.

7 UNITED 3 JUVENTUS 2

1997/98 GROUP STAGE

Beaten home and away by the Italian champions the previous season, United knew that Juve were perhaps the benchmark for elite European football. Conceding inside 30 seconds stunned Old Trafford, but on an unforgettable night the Reds roared back and sealed a momentous victory as Teddy Sheringham equalised, then Paul Scholes and Ryan Giggs sealed the win.

6 PSG 1 UNITED 3

2018/19 SECOND ROUND, SECOND LEG

Having lost 2-0 at Old Trafford, the Reds needed to make history in order to progress past PSG by becoming the first team ever to overcome a home two-goal deficit and go through. Romelu Lukaku's first half brace hauled Ole Gunnar Solskjaer's injury-ravaged side back into the tie, before Marcus Rashford displayed nerves of steel by smashing in a stoppage-time penalty. Unbelievable!

OUR GREATEST CHAMPIONS LEAGUE NIGHTS

5 UNITED 7 ROMA 1

2006/07 QUARTER-FINAL, SECOND LEG

A narrow 2-1 defeat in Rome meant United needed to come out fighting at Old Trafford a week later, but nobody could have imagined the scale of devastation the Reds would inflict! Michael Carrick, Alan Smith, Wayne Rooney and Cristiano Ronaldo ended the tie by half-time, before Ronaldo and Carrick both notched again, as did Patrice Evra, on a barnstorming night in Manchester.

4 UNITED 1 BARCELONA 0

2007/08 SEMI-FINAL, SECOND LEG

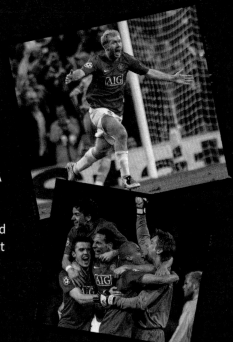

You want tension? Watch the full rerun of this nerve-shredding tie. A goalless draw in the Nou Camp meant that a place in the 2008 final hinged entirely on events at Old Trafford, where just one goal was enough to prove decisive. Thankfully for the Reds, that was provided in spectacular fashion by Paul Scholes' 30-yard piledriver which sent the stadium wild!

3 JUVENTUS 2 UNITED 3

1998/99 SEMI-FINAL, SECOND LEG

Juve were still the Champions League benchmark, aiming to reach a fourth straight final. As such, having drawn 1-1 in Manchester, going 2-0 down in Turin seemed a bold strategy. Instead, the Treble-chasing Reds turned in arguably their greatest ever European performance to fight back and win through goals from Roy Keane, Dwight Yorke and Andy Cole. Magnifico!

2

UNITED 1 CHELSEA 1

(6-5 ON PENALTIES) 2007/08 FINAL

The first all-English Champions League final was a tight, terrifying affair. After Cristiano Ronaldo's brilliant header started the scoring, Frank Lampard tapped in an equaliser. The sides remained level until penalties, and United only avoided defeat when John Terry missed his effort, before Edwin van der Sar saved from Nicolas Anelka to secure a third European rule for the Reds.

1

UNITED 2 BAYERN MUNICH 1

1998/99 FINAL

On probably the greatest evening in United's history, the Reds trailed Mario Basler's early free-kick until stoppage time. Then, two goals in three injury-time minutes from substitutes Teddy Sheringham and Ole Gunnar Solskjaer wrapped up an astonishing turnaround, sealed the Treble and made Alex Ferguson's men European champions. Oh, what a night!

ALWAYS UNITED

MORE THAN A GAME

This is how the Reds set the standard for football clubs during the global pandemic…

In March 2020, football came to a halt as the world struggled to cope with the COVID-19 pandemic. During that three-month break in action, Manchester United stepped up and showed the kind of compassion and generosity the world needed, helping out those in need wherever possible. Our club did us all proud, and here's how they did it…

DONATED 60,000 MEALS TO NHS STAFF AT HOSPITALS IN MANCHESTER AND SALFORD.

GAVE MEDICAL SUPPLIES AND PROTECTIVE EQUIPMENT TO THE NHS.

OPENED UP OLD TRAFFORD'S CAR PARKS TO BE USED FOR SAFE CORONAVIRUS TESTING AREAS.

DONATED HUNDREDS OF THOUSANDS OF POUNDS, PLUS FOOD PARCELS, TO VULNERABLE FAMILIES.

PROVIDED £300,000 TO LOCAL SCHOOLS AND COLLEGES.

SET ASIDE ANOTHER £240,000 FOR SUPPORTERS' CLUBS TO DONATE TO YOUTH-FOCUSED CHARITIES.

OFFERED THE USE OF 16 CLUB VEHICLES FOR THE NHS TO USE TO COURIER SUPPLIES AROUND MANCHESTER.

THAT TOTALLED OVER £1 MILLION OF DONATIONS THROUGH MANCHESTER UNITED FOUNDATION, BUT IT DIDN'T STOP THERE...

CLUB STAFF'S JOBS WERE PROTECTED AND SUPPORT WAS CONSTANTLY OFFERED.

NEARLY 150 MEMBERS OF CLUB STAFF SPENT PART OF LOCKDOWN VOLUNTEERING TO HELP THE NHS.

FORMER PLAYERS INCLUDING BRYAN ROBSON RANG VULNERABLE SUPPORTERS FOR MORALE-BOOSTING CHATS.

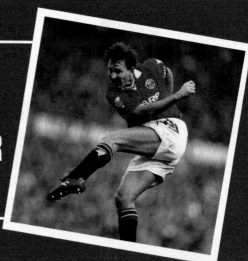

AND AS FOR THE PLAYERS...

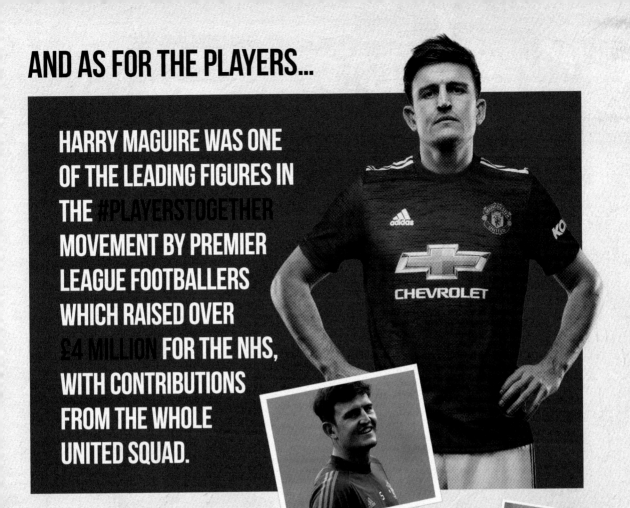

HARRY MAGUIRE WAS ONE OF THE LEADING FIGURES IN THE #PLAYERSTOGETHER MOVEMENT BY PREMIER LEAGUE FOOTBALLERS WHICH RAISED OVER £4 MILLION FOR THE NHS, WITH CONTRIBUTIONS FROM THE WHOLE UNITED SQUAD.

MARCUS RASHFORD WORKED WITH THE BRILLIANT FARESHARE CHARITY TO HELP RAISE OVER £20 MILLION TO PROVIDE FREE SCHOOL MEALS FOR OVER A MILLION CHILDREN WHO WERE GOING HUNGRY DURING LOCKDOWN AND BEYOND — AN UNBELIEVABLE EFFORT!

UNITED ON AND OFF THE PITCH!

QUIZZES & PUZZLES

SPOT THE DIFFERENCE

SCOUR THESE TWO PICTURES AND SEE IF YOU CAN
SPOT THE SIX DIFFERENCES BETWEEN THEM...

ANSWERS ON PAGE 60

```
G  I  G  G  S  B  D  D  Z  N  I  R  W  L  T
J  J  Q  R  F  I  S  N  H  N  M  V  F  R  D
J  Z  T  O  Q  M  O  B  E  S  T  M  L  C  N
N  H  I  O  Z  C  L  L  R  H  N  P  O  O  V
E  U  V  N  T  C  S  K  D  W  U  D  S  L  L
A  G  I  E  M  L  K  I  S  B  L  R  C  E  N
M  H  O  Y  J  A  J  K  F  A  A  Z  A  S  P
O  E  L  M  M  I  A  L  N  E  R  W  S  C  C
S  S  L  P  G  R  E  O  P  N  A  U  S  H  H
W  S  E  Z  X  Y  R  O  Q  L  R  G  I  O  A
Y  M  T  A  Y  L  O  R  V  H  D  S  D  L  R
V  A  N  N  I  S  T  E  L  R  O  O  Y  E  L
G  R  O  W  L  E  Y  W  C  D  B  R  T  S  T
S  K  S  P  E  N  C  E  L  A  X  T  V  T  O
T  U  R  N  B  U  L  L  Z  Q  C  V  V  S  N
```

WORDS GO HORIZONTALLY, VERTICALLY, DIAGONALLY AND BACKWARDS.

ROONEY | CHARLTON | LAW | ROWLEY | VIOLLET | BEST | SPENCE | GIGGS

HUGHES | SCHOLES | VAN NISTELROOY | PEARSON | HERD | TAYLOR

MCCLAIR | SOLSKJAER | COLE | RONALDO | TURNBULL | CASSIDY

EX-REDS IN THE DUGOUT

ALL OF THESE INDIVIDUALS HAVE PREVIOUSLY MANAGED TEAMS AGAINST UNITED – BUT WHICH OF THEM HAVE ALSO REPRESENTED THE REDS AS PLAYERS?

1. MARK HUGHES
2. STEVE BRUCE
3. PEP GUARDIOLA
4. JURGEN KLOPP
5. MAURICIO POCHETTINO
6. ROY KEANE
7. JAAP STAM
8. CARLO ANCELOTTI
9. FRANK LAMPARD
10. MIKE PHELAN

SPOT THE BALL

WHICH OF THESE BALLS HAS ANTHONY MARTIAL JUST KICKED?

WHO MADE MORE APPEARANCES?

WITHIN THESE PAIRS OF PLAYERS, WHICH ONE REPRESENTED THE REDS MORE TIMES?

1 RYAN GIGGS   **OR**   SIR BOBBY CHARLTON

2 DAVID DE GEA   **OR**   PETER SCHMEICHEL

3 WAYNE ROONEY   **OR**   GARY NEVILLE

4 BRYAN ROBSON   **OR**   RIO FERDINAND

5 PAUL INCE   **OR**   ANDY COLE

6 PATRICE EVRA   **OR**   PHIL NEVILLE

7 MICHAEL CARRICK   **OR**   DAVID BECKHAM

8 ROY KEANE   **OR**   GEORGE BEST

9 OLE GUNNAR SOLSKJAER   **OR**   DARREN FLETCHER

10 RUUD VAN NISTELROOY   **OR**   ANTHONY MARTIAL

DEBUTS DOWN THE YEARS

CAN YOU MATCH THESE PLAYERS TO THE YEAR OF THEIR UNITED DEBUT?

1	ZLATAN IBRAHIMOVIC	1973
2	DENIS LAW	1994
3	DWIGHT YORKE	2016
4	DENIS IRWIN	2019
5	LOU MACARI	1962
6	PAUL SCHOLES	1998
7	BRYAN ROBSON	2015
8	CHRIS SMALLING	1990
9	SERGIO ROMERO	1981
10	HARRY MAGUIRE	2010

UNITED'S EUROPEAN TOUR

MATCH THESE OPPOSITION CLUBS TO THE VENUES WHERE THEY
HAVE HOSTED UNITED IN CHAMPIONS LEAGUE ENCOUNTERS...

1	ARSENAL	ESTADIO SANTIAGO BERNABEU
2	AC MILAN	STAMFORD BRIDGE
3	REAL MADRID	STADIO OLIMPICO
4	BARCELONA	PARC DES PRINCES
5	CHELSEA	IBROX
6	ROMA	EMIRATES STADIUM
7	PARIS ST GERMAIN	ARNOLD SCHWARZENEGGER STADIUM
8	RANGERS	SAN SIRO
9	STURM GRAZ	ALLIANZ ARENA
10	BAYERN MUNICH	NOU CAMP

A

B

C

D

GOAL OR NO GOAL?

STUDY THESE 8 IMAGES OF SHOTS ON GOAL UNITED TOOK DURING 2019/20.
CAN YOU REMEMBER WHETHER WE SCORED OR NOT?

E

F

G

H

QUIZ ANSWERS

IT'S TIME TO SEE HOW WELL YOU KNOW UNITED!

SPOT THE DIFFERENCE PAGE 54

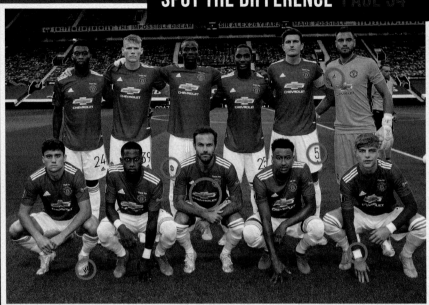

WORDSEARCH PAGE 55

```
G I G G S B D D Z N I R W L T
J J Q R F I S N H N M V F R D
J Z T O Q M O B E S T M L C N
N H I O Z C L L R H N P O O V
E U V N T C S K D W U D S L L
A G I E M L K I S B L R C E N
M H O Y J A J K F A A Z A S P
O E L M M I A L N E R W S C C
S S L P G R E O P N A U S H A
W S E Z X Y R O Q L R G I O R
Y M T A Y L O R V H D S D L E
V A N N I S T E L R O O Y E L
G R O W L E Y W C D B R T S T
S K S P E N C E L A X T V T O
T U R N B U L L Z Q C V V S N
```

EX-REDS IN THE DUGOUT PAGE 56

MARK HUGHES, STEVE BRUCE, ROY KEANE, JAAP STAM AND MIKE PHELAN HAVE ALL BOTH PLAYED FOR AND MANAGED AGAINST UNITED!

WHO MADE MORE APPEARANCES? PAGE 57

1. RYAN GIGGS
2. DAVID DE GEA
3. GARY NEVILLE
4. BRYAN ROBSON
5. PAUL INCE
6. PHIL NEVILLE
7. MICHAEL CARRICK
8. ROY KEANE
9. OLE GUNNAR SOLSKJAER
10. ANTHONY MARTIAL

DEBUTS DOWN THE YEARS PAGE 58

1. DENIS LAW 1962
2. LOU MACARI 1973
3. BRYAN ROBSON 1981
4. DENIS IRWIN 1990
5. PAUL SCHOLES 1994
6. DWIGHT YORKE 1998
7. CHRIS SMALLING 2010
8. SERGIO ROMERO 2015
9. ZLATAN IBRAHIMOVIC 2016
10. HARRY MAGUIRE 2019

UNITED'S EUROPEAN TOUR PAGE 58

1. ARSENAL – EMIRATES STADIUM
2. AC MILAN – SAN SIRO
3. REAL MADRID – ESTADIO SANTIAGO BERNABEU
4. BARCELONA – NOU CAMP
5. CHELSEA – STAMFORD BRIDGE
6. ROMA – STADIO OLIMPICO
7. PARIS ST GERMAIN – PARC DES PRINCES
8. RANGERS – IBROX
9. STURM GRAZ – ARNOLD SCHWARZENEGGER STADIUM
10. BAYERN MUNICH – ALLIANZ ARENA

GOAL OR NO GOAL?

PIC A: GOAL
PIC B: NO GOAL
PIC C: NO GOAL
PIC D: GOAL
PIC E: GOAL
PIC F: GOAL
PIC G: GOAL
PIC H: NO GOAL

PAGE 59

SPOT THE BALL PAGE 56

COMPETITION

BE IN WITH A CHANCE OF WINNING A 2020/21 SHIRT SIGNED BY FIRST TEAM SQUAD MEMBERS

BY ANSWERING THIS ONE SIMPLE QUESTION...

FROM WHICH CLUB DID UNITED SIGN PORTUGUESE MIDFIELDER BRUNO FERNANDES?

A. BENFICA

B. PORTO

C. SPORTING LISBON

VISIT MANUTD.COM/ANNUAL2021 TO ENTER

GOOD LUCK!